AF413637

Age-Appropriate Division Workbook with Word Problems

Math 5th Grade Children's Math Books

Speedy Publishing LLC

40 E. Main St. #1156

Newark, DE 19711

www.speedypublishing.com

Copyright 2017

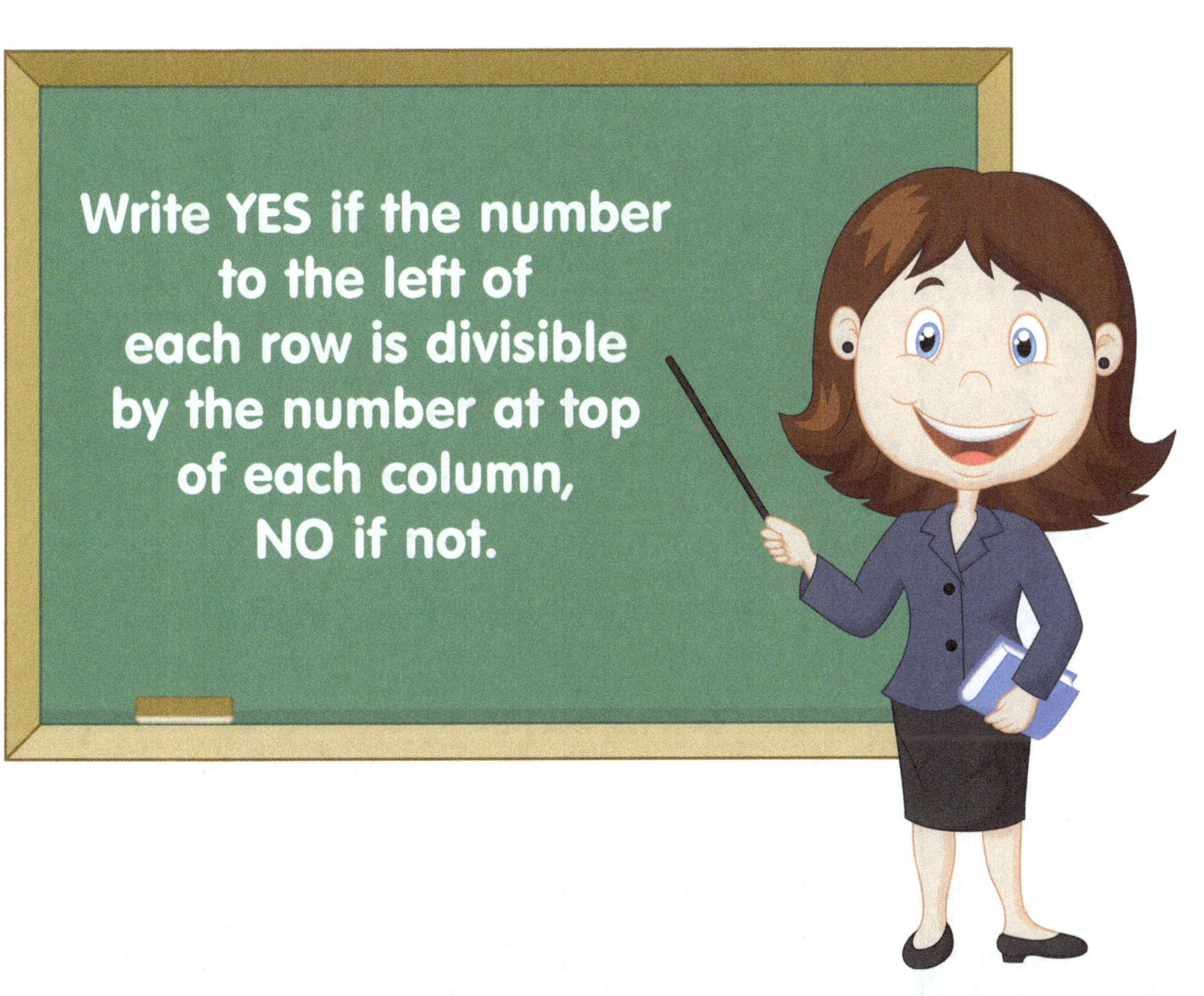

Write YES if the number
to the left of
each row is divisible
by the number at top
of each column,
NO if not.

EXERCISE NO. 1

	2	3	4	5	6	9
54						
18						
91						
84						
63						
44						
86						
68						
38						
10						
88						
87						

EXERCISE NO. 2

	2	3	4	5	6	9
52						
20						
40						
95						
46						
70						
34						
98						
50						
74						
84						
92						

EXERCISE NO. 3

	2	3	4	5	6	9
82						
95						
78						
24						
76						
56						
99						
28						
74						
12						
27						
52						

EXERCISE NO. 4

	2	3	4	5	6	9
35						
84						
87						
10						
34						
96						
90						
42						
14						
80						
39						
44						

EXERCISE NO. 5

	2	3	4	5	6	9
40						
24						
62						
44						
34						
42						
33						
50						
10						
75						
57						
25						

EXERCISE NO. 6

	2	3	4	5	6	9
99						
32						
90						
50						
35						
39						
68						
75						
24						
34						
20						
26						

EXERCISE NO. 7

	2	3	4	5	6	9
50						
14						
75						
80						
46						
48						
55						
18						
10						
60						
34						
16						

EXERCISE NO. 8

	2	3	4	5	6	9
69						
36						
85						
63						
32						
64						
57						
68						
40						
75						
91						
20						

# EXERCISE NO. 9

	2	3	4	5	6	9
903						
836						
542						
585						
573						
618						
670						
564						
360						
882						
565						
867						

EXERCISE NO. 10

	2	3	4	5	6	9
669						
810						
936						
327						
965						
732						
927						
380						
300						
832						
672						
275						

Find the Quotient.

EXERCISE NO. 11

10 ÷ 2 =   36 ÷ 4 =   36 ÷ 3 =

48 ÷ 8 =   28 ÷ 7 =   63 ÷ 9 =

90 ÷ 10 =   16 ÷ 2 =   8 ÷ 1 =

EXERCISE NO. 12

$40 \div 5 =$ $36 \div 6 =$ $120 \div 10 =$

$21 \div 3 =$ $27 \div 9 =$ $28 \div 7 =$

$60 \div 12 =$ $8 \div 1 =$ $18 \div 3 =$

EXERCISE NO. 13

16 ÷ 2 =   24 ÷ 6 =   99 ÷ 11 =

48 ÷ 4 =   108 ÷ 9 =   20 ÷ 10 =

33 ÷ 11 =   49 ÷ 7 =   70 ÷ 10 =

EXERCISE NO. 14

12 ÷ 4 =   60 ÷ 10 =   33 ÷ 3 =

70 ÷ 7 =   99 ÷ 11 =   56 ÷ 7 =

8 ÷ 4 =   12 ÷ 1 =   32 ÷ 8 =

EXERCISE NO. 15

$12 \div 4 =$ $63 \div 9 =$ $100 \div 10 =$

$18 \div 9 =$ $120 \div 12 =$ $33 \div 3 =$

$8 \div 1 =$ $15 \div 3 =$ $72 \div 6 =$

EXERCISE NO. 16

30 ÷ 10 =   54 ÷ 6 =   11 ÷ 1 =

2 ÷ 1 =   100 ÷ 10 =   72 ÷ 12 =

9 ÷ 9 =   63 ÷ 9 =   88 ÷ 11 =

EXERCISE NO. 17

144 ÷ 12 =   88 ÷ 8 =   40 ÷ 10 =

7 ÷ 7 =   88 ÷ 11 =   40 ÷ 5 =

42 ÷ 6 =   18 ÷ 9 =   9 ÷ 1 =

EXERCISE NO. 18

36 ÷ 3 =   40 ÷ 4 =   9 ÷ 1 =

88 ÷ 11 =   30 ÷ 5 =   132 ÷ 12 =

48 ÷ 12 =   48 ÷ 4 =   77 ÷ 7 =

EXERCISE NO. 19

72 ÷ 9 =   36 ÷ 12 =   120 ÷ 10 =

3 ÷ 3 =   18 ÷ 2 =   7 ÷ 7 =

56 ÷ 8 =   48 ÷ 12 =   30 ÷ 5 =

# EXERCISE NO. 20

16 ÷ 2 =   20 ÷ 5 =   55 ÷ 5 =

6 ÷ 6 =   45 ÷ 9 =   5 ÷ 1 =

77 ÷ 11 =   110 ÷ 11 =   64 ÷ 8 =

$$4 \overline{)2360} \qquad 3 \overline{)789} \qquad 7 \overline{)4305}$$

$$7 \overline{)6559} \qquad 7 \overline{)4263} \qquad 5 \overline{)3755}$$

$$4 \overline{)3084} \qquad 4 \overline{)908} \qquad 6 \overline{)1620}$$

EXERCISE NO. 22

$8\overline{)256}$ $3\overline{)243}$ $6\overline{)84}$

$3\overline{)282}$ $7\overline{)287}$ $3\overline{)102}$

$3\overline{)48}$ $4\overline{)340}$ $7\overline{)273}$

EXERCISE NO. 23

$8\overline{)312}$ $9\overline{)846}$ $5\overline{)280}$

$8\overline{)696}$ $5\overline{)360}$ $6\overline{)126}$

$7\overline{)518}$ $2\overline{)44}$ $7\overline{)357}$

$3\overline{)57}$ $3\overline{)243}$ $2\overline{)152}$

$8\overline{)488}$ $7\overline{)602}$ $2\overline{)68}$

$9\overline{)747}$ $6\overline{)168}$ $9\overline{)513}$

Read and answer
each word problem
carefully.

A restaurant sold 42 hamburgers last week.
How many hamburgers on average were sold each day ?

Jason has 60 cents in his bank.
How many dimes does Jason have ?

There were a total of 18 football games during the three month season.
If the games are equally divided, how many football games are played a month ?

Joan, Sandy, and Jessica have 18 crayons all together.
If the crayons are equally divided, how many will each person get ?

EXERCISE NO. 26

Tim has 15 dollars in five dollar bills. How many five dollars bills does he have ?

Sally has 30 cents in her bank.
How many dimes does Sally have ?

There were a total of 9 hockey games during the three month season.
If the games are equally divided, how many hockey games are played a month ?

Tim worked 15 hours in the last five days. Assuming that he worked the same amount of hours each day, how long did he work each day ?

EXERCISE NO. 27

Sandy has 36 blue balloons. She wants to give her six friends the same number of blue balloons, how many will each friend get ?

Sam, Benny, and Jason have 18 erasers all together.
If the erasers are equally divided, how many will each person get ?

Mary worked 30 hours in the last five days. Assuming that she worked the same amount of hours each day, how long did she work each day ?

Melanie was at the beach for five days and found 24 seashells.
She plans to give all of her seashells equally to her four friends.
How many seashells will each friend get ?

EXERCISE NO. 28

Sally worked 20 hours in the last five days. Assuming that she worked the same amount of hours each day, how long did she work each day ?

There were a total of 12 hockey games during the three month season.
If the games are equally divided, how many hockey games are played a month ?

Mary was at the beach for five days and found 16 seashells.
She plans to give all of her seashells equally to her four friends.
How many seashells will each friend get ?

Jessica has 40 cents in her bank.
How many dimes does Jessica have ?

EXERCISE NO. 29

Sam worked 15 hours in the last five days. Assuming that he worked the same amount of hours each day, how long did he work each day ?

Sandy has 30 cents in her bank.
How many dimes does Sandy have ?

Keith has 15 dollars in five dollar bills. How many five dollars bills does he have ?

Melanie goes fishing with Fred. They catch 6 trout.
If they equally split up the trout, how may will each one get ?

EXERCISE NO. 30

Jason has 90 cents in his bank.
How many dimes does Jason have ?

Dan, Nancy, and Tom have 27 pencils all together.
If the pencils are equally divided, how many will each person get ?

There were a total of 27 soccer games during the three month season.
If the games are equally divided, how many soccer games are played a month ?

A restaurant sold 63 hot dogs last week.
How many hot dogs on average were sold each day ?

# EXERCISE NO. 31

Sandy worked 45 hours in the last five days. Assuming that she worked the same amount of hours each day, how long did she work each day ?

Sam has 54 green balloons. He wants to give his six friends the same number of green balloons, how many will each friend get ?

Mike goes fishing with Sam. They catch 18 trout.
If they equally split up the trout, how may will each one get ?

Dan was at the beach for five days and found 36 seashells.
He plans to give all of his seashells equally to his four friends.
How many seashells will each friend get ?

EXERCISE NO. 32

Tim worked 35 hours in the last five days. Assuming that he worked the same amount of hours each day, how long did he work each day ?

Joan goes out to lunch with Tim and Mike. The total bill came to 18 dollars. They decided to equally split up the bill, how much will each person have to pay ?

Mike, Joan, and Alyssa have 21 crayons all together.
If the crayons are equally divided, how many will each person get ?

Jessica has 42 violet balloons. She wants to give her six friends the same number of violet balloons, how many will each friend get ?

EXERCISE NO. 33

Jessica has 15 dollars in five dollar bills. How many five dollars bills does she have ?

Sam goes fishing with Alyssa. They catch 6 trout.
If they equally split up the trout, how may will each one get ?

Alyssa was at the beach for five days and found 12 seashells.
She plans to give all of her seashells equally to her four friends.
How many seashells will each friend get ?

Benny goes out to lunch with Nancy and Jason. The total bill came to 24 dollars.
They decided to equally split up the bill, how much will each person have to pay ?

EXERCISE NO. 34

Mary worked 40 hours in the last five days. Assuming that she worked the same amount of hours each day, how long did she work each day ?

Keith goes out to lunch with Jessica and Sandy. The total bill came to 21 dollars. They decided to equally split up the bill, how much will each person have to pay ?

A restaurant sold 56 sandwiches last week.
How many sandwiches on average were sold each day ?

Sam has 40 dollars in five dollar bills. How many five dollars bills does he have ?

EXERCISE NO. 35

Jason has 96 blue marbles. Sam has 3 times more blue marbles than Jason. How many dozen blue marbles does Sam have?

Tim has saved 9 dollars from washing cars.
How many dozen quarters does Tim have?

Tim, Joan, Nancy, and Melanie each have 12 baseball cards.
How many dozen baseball cards do they have in all?

Joan bought 72 eggs from the store to bake some cakes.
How many dozen eggs did Joan buy?

EXERCISE NO. 36

Keith has 84 blue marbles. Mary has 4 times more blue marbles than Keith. How many dozen blue marbles does Mary have?

Melanie saw 48 birds in a tree.
How many dozen birds did Melanie see?

Melanie, Sally, Benny, and Fred each have 12 Pokemon cards.
How many dozen Pokemon cards do they have in all?

There are 19 children in a class, and each student has 36 pencils. How many dozen pencils are there in all?

# EXERCISE NO. 37

There are 42 children in a class, and each student has 24 pencils. How many dozen pencils are there in all?

Jason earns $25.00 for each house he cleans. If he cleans 96 houses, how many dozens of dollars will he make?

Tim has 72 books. Keith has 8 times more books than Tim. How many dozen books does Keith have?

Mike saw 96 birds in a tree.
How many dozen birds did Mike see?

EXERCISE NO. 38

Melanie has 180 golf balls.
How many dozen golf balls does she have?

Melanie saw 84 birds in a tree.
How many dozen birds did Melanie see?

Melanie has saved 18 dollars from washing cars.
How many dozen quarters does Melanie have?

Dan has 36 blue marbles. Sally has 7 times more blue marbles
than Dan. How many dozen blue marbles does Sally have?

EXERCISE NO. 39

Mary has 84 blue marbles. Sally has 2 times more blue marbles than Mary. How many dozen blue marbles does Sally have?

Sam has 24 books. Dan has 2 times more books than Sam. How many dozen books does Dan have?

Benny, Mike, Joan, and Dan each have 60 Pokemon cards. How many dozen Pokemon cards do they have in all?

Melanie earns $25.00 for each house she cleans. If she cleans 48 houses, how many dozens of dollars will she make?

EXERCISE NO. 40

Benny bought 12 eggs from the store to bake some cakes.
How many dozen eggs did Benny buy?

Sally, Benny, Sandy, and Jason each have 60 Pokemon cards.
How many dozen Pokemon cards do they have in all?

Sally has saved 24 dollars from washing cars.
How many dozen quarters does Sally have?

Alyssa earns $25.00 for each house she cleans. If she cleans
48 houses, how many dozens of dollars will she make?

EXERCISE NO. 41

Joan saw 24 birds in a tree.
How many dozen birds did Joan see?

Tom has 24 blue marbles. Sara has 2 times more blue marbles
than Tom. How many dozen blue marbles does Sara have?

Tim has 96 books. Jessica has 2 times more books than
Tim. How many dozen books does Jessica have?

Joan has 204 golf balls.
How many dozen golf balls does she have?

EXERCISE NO. 42

Tim saw 96 birds in a tree.
How many dozen birds did Tim see?

Tom earns $25.00 for each house he cleans. If he cleans
96 houses, how many dozens of dollars will he make?

There are 84 calories in a candy bar. How many
dozen calories are there in 43 candy bars?

There are 43 children in a class, and each student has 24
pencils. How many dozen pencils are there in all?

EXERCISE NO. 43

Fred saw 72 birds in a tree.
How many dozen birds did Fred see?

Keith bought 72 eggs from the store to bake some cakes.
How many dozen eggs did Keith buy?

Sam has 12 blue marbles. Mary has 6 times more blue marbles
than Sam. How many dozen blue marbles does Mary have?

Benny has 60 books. Mike has 6 times more books than
Benny. How many dozen books does Mike have?

EXERCISE NO. 44

Melanie has 216 golf balls.
How many dozen golf balls does she have?

Melanie has saved 15 dollars from washing cars.
How many dozen quarters does Melanie have?

There are 29 children in a class, and each student has 24 pencils. How many dozen pencils are there in all?

Melanie saw 60 birds in a tree.
How many dozen birds did Melanie see?

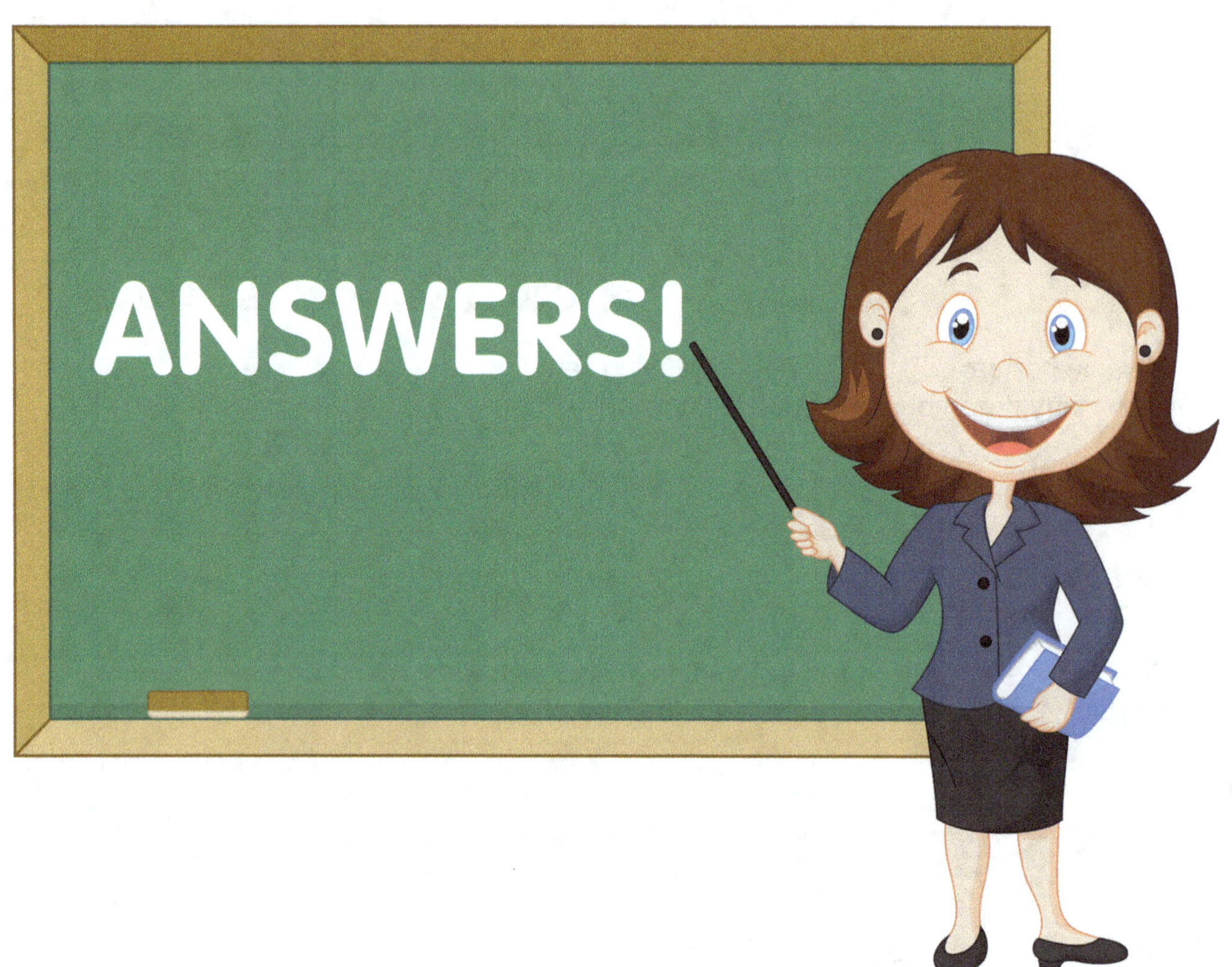
ANSWERS!

	2	3	4	5	6	9
54	YES	YES	NO	NO	YES	YES
18	YES	YES	NO	NO	YES	YES
91	NO	NO	NO	NO	NO	NO
84	YES	YES	YES	NO	YES	NO
63	NO	YES	NO	NO	NO	YES
44	YES	NO	YES	NO	NO	NO
86	YES	NO	NO	NO	NO	NO
68	YES	NO	YES	NO	NO	NO
38	YES	NO	NO	NO	NO	NO
10	YES	NO	NO	YES	NO	NO
88	YES	NO	YES	NO	NO	NO
87	NO	YES	NO	NO	NO	NO

	2	3	4	5	6	9
52	YES	NO	YES	NO	NO	NO
20	YES	NO	YES	YES	NO	NO
40	YES	NO	YES	YES	NO	NO
95	NO	NO	NO	YES	NO	NO
46	YES	NO	NO	NO	NO	NO
70	YES	YES	NO	YES	NO	NO
34	YES	NO	NO	NO	NO	NO
98	YES	NO	NO	NO	NO	NO
50	YES	NO	NO	YES	NO	NO
74	YES	NO	NO	NO	NO	NO
84	YES	YES	YES	NO	YES	NO
92	YES	NO	YES	NO	NO	NO

	2	3	4	5	6	9
82	YES	NO	NO	NO	NO	NO
95	NO	NO	NO	YES	NO	NO
78	YES	YES	NO	NO	YES	NO
24	YES	YES	YES	NO	YES	NO
76	YES	NO	YES	NO	NO	NO
56	YES	NO	YES	NO	NO	NO
99	NO	YES	NO	NO	NO	YES
28	YES	NO	YES	NO	NO	NO
74	YES	NO	NO	NO	NO	NO
12	YES	YES	YES	NO	YES	NO
27	NO	YES	NO	NO	NO	YES
52	YES	NO	YES	NO	NO	NO

	2	3	4	5	6	9
35	NO	NO	NO	YES	NO	NO
84	YES	YES	YES	NO	YES	NO
87	NO	YES	NO	NO	NO	NO
10	YES	NO	NO	YES	NO	NO
34	YES	NO	NO	NO	NO	NO
96	YES	YES	YES	NO	YES	NO
90	YES	YES	NO	YES	YES	YES
42	YES	YES	NO	NO	YES	NO
14	YES	NO	NO	NO	NO	NO
80	YES	NO	YES	YES	NO	NO
39	NO	YES	NO	NO	NO	NO
44	YES	NO	YES	NO	NO	NO

EXERCISE NO. 5

	2	3	4	5	6	9
40	YES	NO	YES	YES	NO	NO
24	YES	YES	YES	NO	YES	NO
62	YES	NO	NO	NO	NO	NO
44	YES	NO	YES	NO	NO	NO
34	YES	NO	NO	NO	NO	NO
42	YES	YES	NO	NO	YES	NO
33	NO	YES	NO	NO	NO	NO
50	YES	NO	NO	YES	NO	NO
10	YES	NO	NO	YES	NO	NO
75	NO	YES	NO	YES	NO	NO
57	NO	YES	NO	NO	NO	NO
25	NO	NO	NO	YES	NO	NO

EXERCISE NO. 6

	2	3	4	5	6	9
99	NO	YES	NO	NO	NO	YES
32	YES	NO	YES	NO	NO	NO
90	YES	YES	NO	YES	YES	YES
50	YES	NO	NO	YES	NO	NO
35	NO	NO	NO	YES	NO	NO
39	NO	YES	NO	NO	NO	NO
68	YES	NO	YES	NO	NO	NO
75	NO	YES	NO	YES	NO	NO
24	YES	YES	YES	NO	YES	NO
34	YES	NO	NO	NO	NO	NO
20	YES	NO	YES	YES	NO	NO
26	YES	NO	NO	NO	NO	NO

EXERCISE NO. 7

	2	3	4	5	6	9
50	YES	NO	NO	YES	NO	NO
14	YES	NO	NO	NO	NO	NO
75	NO	YES	NO	YES	NO	NO
80	YES	NO	YES	YES	NO	NO
46	YES	NO	NO	NO	NO	NO
48	YES	YES	YES	NO	YES	NO
55	NO	NO	NO	YES	NO	NO
18	YES	YES	NO	NO	YES	YES
10	YES	NO	NO	YES	NO	NO
60	YES	YES	YES	YES	YES	NO
34	YES	NO	NO	NO	NO	NO
16	YES	NO	YES	NO	NO	NO

EXERCISE NO. 8

	2	3	4	5	6	9
69	NO	YES	NO	NO	NO	NO
36	YES	YES	YES	NO	YES	YES
85	NO	NO	NO	YES	NO	NO
63	NO	YES	NO	NO	NO	YES
32	YES	NO	YES	NO	NO	NO
64	YES	NO	YES	NO	NO	NO
57	NO	YES	NO	NO	NO	NO
68	YES	NO	YES	NO	NO	NO
40	YES	NO	YES	YES	NO	NO
75	NO	YES	NO	YES	NO	NO
91	NO	NO	NO	NO	NO	NO
20	YES	NO	YES	YES	NO	NO

EXERCISE NO. 9

	2	3	4	5	6	9
903	NO	YES	NO	NO	NO	NO
836	YES	NO	YES	NO	NO	NO
542	YES	NO	NO	NO	NO	NO
585	NO	YES	NO	YES	NO	YES
573	NO	YES	NO	NO	NO	NO
618	YES	YES	NO	NO	YES	NO
670	YES	NO	NO	YES	NO	NO
564	YES	YES	YES	NO	YES	NO
360	YES	YES	YES	YES	YES	YES
882	YES	YES	NO	NO	YES	YES
565	NO	NO	NO	YES	NO	NO
867	NO	YES	NO	NO	NO	NO

EXERCISE NO. 10

	2	3	4	5	6	9
669	NO	YES	NO	NO	NO	NO
810	YES	YES	NO	YES	YES	YES
936	YES	YES	YES	NO	YES	YES
327	NO	YES	NO	NO	NO	NO
965	NO	NO	NO	YES	NO	NO
732	YES	YES	YES	NO	YES	NO
927	NO	YES	NO	NO	NO	YES
380	YES	NO	YES	YES	NO	NO
300	YES	YES	YES	YES	YES	NO
832	YES	NO	YES	NO	NO	NO
672	YES	YES	YES	NO	YES	NO
275	NO	NO	NO	YES	NO	NO

EXERCISE NO. 11

10 ÷ 2 = 5	36 ÷ 4 = 9	36 ÷ 3 = 12
48 ÷ 8 = 6	28 ÷ 7 = 4	63 ÷ 9 = 7
90 ÷ 10 = 9	16 ÷ 2 = 8	8 ÷ 1 = 8

EXERCISE NO. 12

40 ÷ 5 = 8	36 ÷ 6 = 6	120 ÷ 10 = 12
21 ÷ 3 = 7	27 ÷ 9 = 3	28 ÷ 7 = 4
60 ÷ 12 = 5	8 ÷ 1 = 8	18 ÷ 3 = 6

16 ÷ 2 = 8   24 ÷ 6 = 4   99 ÷ 11 = 9

48 ÷ 4 = 12   108 ÷ 9 = 12   20 ÷ 10 = 2

33 ÷ 11 = 3   49 ÷ 7 = 7   70 ÷ 10 = 7

12 ÷ 4 = 3   60 ÷ 10 = 6   33 ÷ 3 = 11

70 ÷ 7 = 10   99 ÷ 11 = 9   56 ÷ 7 = 8

8 ÷ 4 = 2   12 ÷ 1 = 12   32 ÷ 8 = 4

12 ÷ 4 = 3   63 ÷ 9 = 7   100 ÷ 10 = 10

18 ÷ 9 = 2   120 ÷ 12 = 10   33 ÷ 3 = 11

8 ÷ 1 = 8   15 ÷ 3 = 5   72 ÷ 6 = 12

30 ÷ 10 = 3   54 ÷ 6 = 9   11 ÷ 1 = 11

2 ÷ 1 = 2   100 ÷ 10 = 10   72 ÷ 12 = 6

9 ÷ 9 = 1   63 ÷ 9 = 7   88 ÷ 11 = 8

144 ÷ 12 = 12   88 ÷ 8 = 11   40 ÷ 10 = 4

7 ÷ 7 = 1   88 ÷ 11 = 8   40 ÷ 5 = 8

42 ÷ 6 = 7   18 ÷ 9 = 2   9 ÷ 1 = 9

36 ÷ 3 = 12   40 ÷ 4 = 10   9 ÷ 1 = 9

88 ÷ 11 = 8   30 ÷ 5 = 6   132 ÷ 12 = 11

48 ÷ 12 = 4   48 ÷ 4 = 12   77 ÷ 7 = 11

72 ÷ 9 = 8   36 ÷ 12 = 3   120 ÷ 10 = 12

3 ÷ 3 = 1   18 ÷ 2 = 9   7 ÷ 7 = 1

56 ÷ 8 = 7   48 ÷ 12 = 4   30 ÷ 5 = 6

16 ÷ 2 = 8   20 ÷ 5 = 4   55 ÷ 5 = 11

6 ÷ 6 = 1   45 ÷ 9 = 5   5 ÷ 1 = 5

77 ÷ 11 = 7   110 ÷ 11 = 10   64 ÷ 8 = 8

590 $4\overline{)2360}$	263 $3\overline{)789}$	615 $7\overline{)4305}$
937 $7\overline{)6559}$	609 $7\overline{)4263}$	751 $5\overline{)3755}$
771 $4\overline{)3084}$	227 $4\overline{)908}$	270 $6\overline{)1620}$

32 $8\overline{)256}$	81 $3\overline{)243}$	14 $6\overline{)84}$
94 $3\overline{)282}$	41 $7\overline{)287}$	34 $3\overline{)102}$
16 $3\overline{)48}$	85 $4\overline{)340}$	39 $7\overline{)273}$

39 $8\overline{)312}$	94 $9\overline{)846}$	56 $5\overline{)280}$
87 $8\overline{)696}$	72 $5\overline{)360}$	21 $6\overline{)126}$
74 $7\overline{)518}$	22 $2\overline{)44}$	51 $7\overline{)357}$

19 $3\overline{)57}$	81 $3\overline{)243}$	76 $2\overline{)152}$
61 $8\overline{)488}$	86 $7\overline{)602}$	34 $2\overline{)68}$
83 $9\overline{)747}$	28 $6\overline{)168}$	57 $9\overline{)513}$

EXERCISE NO. 25

6 hamburgers

6 dimes

6 games

6 crayons

EXERCISE NO. 26

3 five dollars bills

3 dimes

3 games

3 hours

EXERCISE NO. 27

6 blue balloons

6 erasers

6 hours

6 seashells

EXERCISE NO. 28

4 hours

4 games

4 seashells

4 dimes

3 hours _______________

3 dimes _______________

3 five dollars bills _______________

3 trout _______________

9 dimes _______________

9 pencils _______________

9 games _______________

9 hot dogs _______________

9 hours _______________

9 green balloons _______________

9 trout _______________

9 seashells _______________

7 hours _______________

6 dollars _______________

7 crayons _______________

7 violet balloons _______________

EXERCISE NO. 33

3 five dollars bills

3 trout

3 seashells

8 dollars

EXERCISE NO. 34

8 hours

7 dollars

8 sandwiches

8 five dollars bills

EXERCISE NO. 35

24 dozen blue marbles

8 dozen quarters

4 dozen baseball cards

6 dozen eggs

EXERCISE NO. 36

28 dozen blue marbles

4 dozen birds

4 dozen Pokemon cards

57 dozen pencils

EXERCISE NO. 37

84 dozen pencils

200 dozen dollars

48 dozen books

8 dozen birds

EXERCISE NO. 38

15 dozen golf balls

7 dozen birds

5 dozen quarters

21 dozen blue marbles

EXERCISE NO. 39

14 dozen blue marbles

4 dozen books

20 dozen Pokemon cards

100 dozen dollars

EXERCISE NO. 40

1 dozen eggs

20 dozen Pokemon cards

1 dozen quarters

100 dozen dollars

EXERCISE NO. 41

2 dozen birds

4 dozen blue marbles

16 dozen books

17 dozen golf balls

EXERCISE NO. 42

8 dozen birds

200 dozen dollars

301 dozen calories

86 dozen pencils

EXERCISE NO. 43

6 dozen birds

6 dozen eggs

6 dozen blue marbles

30 dozen books

EXERCISE NO. 44

18 dozen golf balls

6 dozen quarters

58 dozen pencils

5 dozen birds

Visit

BABY PROFESSOR
EDUCATION KIDS

www.BabyProfessorBooks.com

to download Free Baby Professor eBooks and view
our catalog of new and exciting Children's Books